BLUFF YOUR WAY IN SEX

TIM WEBB & SARAH BREWER

Ravette London

Published by Ravette Limited
3 Glenside Estate, Star Road,
Partridge Green, Horsham,
Sussex RH13 8RA
(0403) 710392

Series Editor – Anne Tauté

Cover design – Jim Wire
Typesetting – Input Typesetting Ltd
Printing & Binding – Cox & Wyman Ltd.
Production – Oval Projects Ltd.

The Bluffer's Guides are based on
an original idea by Peter Wolfe.

CONTENTS

INTRODUCTION

To get the whole sex thing in proportion (and to amaze your friends at parties), contemplate that every second which passes bears witness world-wide to 18,000 male orgasms. Put another way, at any one moment there are likely to be six million human beings actively involved in the sexual appreciation of someone else's body. And that is excluding the ones actively appreciating their own.

If you compare the above figure with the international birth rate of 4.4 I.P.S. (infants per second) then the hypothesis that humans copulate so as to procreate becomes patently ludicrous. Certainly the ratio of product output to unit of energy input would not impress most monetarists. Perhaps because most monetarists gave up such worldly pleasures years ago.

Sex has numerous advantages over other pastimes. It is cheaper than golf or tennis because the main equipment is free. Sex is less skilful than, say, snooker, though that is not to say that both games cannot be improved by practice and sheer hard work. There is more immediate satisfaction to sex than there is in philately or in listening to Radio 4. And you don't have to gather as many players as you would for a cricket match.

Perhaps it is because it is such a simple, pleasurable and generally harmless activity that it has come in for so much stick over the centuries. You need only refer to the most basic historical texts to see that all the great leaders, especially those proved in later years to be misguided bumbling despots, propounded policies which included less sex for the masses. Indeed, to spot a modern day dictator we recommend you to seek out their views on illicit nooky.

In years gone by the situation was simple. Sex was something which was done. It happened rather like eating and sleeping and breathing and passing wind. The fact that everyone else did it too was a comfort, not a threat, so discussion was minimal and confined to barrack huts, public bars and other places of limited sexual activity, where fantastic claims and counter-claims were made, unhindered by reality.

The advent of penicillin, effective contraception, Cosmopolitan and the Ford Escort XR 3i have changed all that forever.

A mature understanding of sexual mores (and nifty new ways of doing it) is not only acceptable but is a mandatory qualification for admission into some social circles.

The aim of our text is to provide you with all the information you may require to bluff your way to the bottom.

So to speak.

THE FACTS

A cursory look at the design and anatomical positioning of the male and female sexual organs shows that when God designed homo sapiens, aestheticism and ease of access were not high on the job description. The human genitalia are not user-friendly.

It is interesting to speculate how more secular engineers might have tackled the task. Brunel, for example, would have foreseen the mechanical stresses which the male's thrusting action places on an already overloaded spinal column. Da Vinci would undoubtedly have made better use of the navel. Maybe he did. It might explain the smile on the Mona Lisa.

The Male

The Penis

The **penis** is known by dozens of pseudonyms, none of which is half as funny as the puritanically po-faced word 'penis' itself. It is one of the Creator's better jokes that the straggling fleshy afterthought which hangs from a man like the knotted rubber blow-hole on a half-dead Boxing Day balloon, is the tool by which he shall reproduce his own kind.

The key to the design is the use of an inflatable bung. Having a dual function is not easy for an organ but the bung makes this possible. The flaccid penis can be peed through but ejaculation is highly unlikely because as soon as the male is sexually stimulated the inflatable bung fills up with blood, the organ expands, stiffens and as if by magic the draining mechanism is cut off, sustaining erection, and the original urinary function of the organ becomes seriously impaired.

The average size of the erect penis is 6½ inches when measured from tip to base with a straight ruler on the side with the wiggly vein. The variation in size is far less than the men's magazines would have us believe, 95 per cent of all men falling between the extreme of 5.8 and 7.0 inches. Claims on the walls of public conveniences throughout the western world may be safely ignored.

The Testes

Literally 'the witnesses', a Latin joke foisted on the world by prudish mediaeval wits of the medical profession. Known in almost every culture as 'balls', though until the invention of the game of Rugby the acronym was slightly inaccurate as the organs are egg-shaped.

Whilst the penis takes the limelight it is the **testes** which do most of the serious work, such as churning out sperm by the billion and regulating the outflow of miniscule amounts of sex drive hormones into the blood. Romantic lovers might work best in the warm, but testes prefer it cold, which explains why they hang down from the body in an adjustable bag.

The Tubes

The testes are plumbed into the penis by two lengths of tubing with immensely complicated names like vas deferens, epididymus and urethra. The system has more side canals and blind alleys than Venice. Some ancient anatomists like **Cowper**, who spent decades dissecting the parts of male corpses, have their reward in the dubious immortality gained by giving one's name to unpleasant but irrelevant glands somewhere deep in the plumbing.

The Female

The Breasts

Breast size is determined by genetic endowment and something awfully complicated happening around the time of adolescence with one's hormone levels. There is strong evidence that an obsession with mammary tissue predates the invention of *The Sun*. However, unlike rounded haunches and slender legs, breasts are not acknowledged as being sexually appealing in either the Bible or the Koran. In many 'undeveloped' cultures breasts are on an erotic par with hairstyle or shape of lips. European art from the Renaissance to the mid 19th century suggests a similar attitude.

One of the world's leading brassière manufacturers grades breasts in four sizes: 'Ping Pong', 'Ding Dong', 'King Kong' and 'Holy Cow'.

There is no doubt that breast size and shape is subject to changing fashion. Pity the poor British woman born during the Second World War. In 1963, for her, large breasts were compulsory, by 1967 they had to be worn bra-less and by 1969 they had to have disappeared altogether.

Male readers obsessed with breast size are advised to seek the assistance of a Freudian psychoanalyst specialising in Oedipal conflicts.

The Vagina

That part of the female anatomy whose external appearance resembles Che Guevara's beard with a vertical smile.

Mediaeval medical wits derived this name from the Latin word for the halter in which a Roman legionnaire stuck his sword.

Erotic artists from earlier eras maximised the sensual appeal of this part of a woman's body by keeping it out of sight. The casual observer of the more direct approach of modern day porn will see why.

Generations of patients refer to the vagina as 'the front passage' for reasons best known to their collective self. In fact it is not so much a passage as a cul de sac with a tiny exit at the top end into the neck (**cervix**) of the usually disinterested and intransigent womb (**uterus**).

The Internal Organs:

The working parts of a woman's reproductive anatomy look, in vertical cross-section, rather like the silhouette of King Kong hovering over New York in the classic silent version of the movie.

The great ape's body represents the womb, to which any of us who has so much as bitten the odd fingernail is said to be pining to return. The walls of the uterus are made of strong muscle with a disposable lining of cellular velvet. To put things in proportion, if a woman's bladder had muscular capabilities as advanced as her uterus, then from a supine position she could pee over St. Pauls.

King Kong's arms represent the **Fallopian tubes** down which passes the occasional egg, up which passes the occasional nasty, tube-blocking infection and across which strikes the gynaecologist's sterilising clips. At the end of each arm, clutched delicately in the fingertips is an effete and tetchy **ovary**. It is this pair of petulant organs which is responsible for spitting out a tiny human egg every month or two and manufacturing some of the hormones which regulate a woman's pre-menstrual tension, post-natal depression, menopausal hot flushes, irregular painful periods and, very occasionally, a normal menstrual cycle.

How It All Works

Hormones
Hormones are remarkably clever chemicals which ooze into the bloodstream from a number of different glands. They can make the body do a wide variety of extraordinary things.

Female hormones come in five basic types and control fertility, sexual development, pregnancy, milk yield and, to a limited extent, mood and frumpiness. Male hormones are all variations on a single theme and control hairiness, sex drive, genital formation and, to a limited extent aggression and frumpiness. All men have female hormones floating around inside them and all women, whether or not they wish to become Olympic discus throwers, have male hormones.

Because they are such subtle items you need not bother to learn about hormones other than to respect them as being mind-bogglingly complicated and 'not fully understood'.

Libido
The coy term for sex drive. This varies enormously from person to person and from day to day, if not hour on hour. The cause of sex drive is unknown. Women are advised that physique and fitness are rarely determinants of sexual prowess in a man. Impotence is as common in boxers as it is in bank clerks. Short men should take heart from the fact that a few years ago

the star of the Stockholm stage was an achondroplastic dwarf with a runaway libido, and turbo charged performance.

Pheromones

One of the better inventions of the 20th century. The theory goes that all mammals secrete tiny amounts of smelly substances called **pheromones**. The combinations vary infinitely from species to species and from individual to individual.

In the brief period since their 'discovery' they have been held responsible, rightly or wrongly, for sexual attractiveness, success at interviews, maintaining true love, goading tribal behaviour such as football violence and many other mysteries of the modern age. To a pheromone freak kissing is clandestine sniffing, copulation is an orgy of aromas and Chanel No. 5 is the social equivalent of mustard gas.

There may turn out to be a scientific basis to the claim that they affect sexual attractiveness. Wizened old lady chimpanzees who would normally have to make do with the odd banana, when sprayed with chimp pheromone instantly become the centre of attention of the virile young males. Ageing Hollywood sex symbols have been known to attempt something similar using musk oil and Grecian 2000.

Orgasms

Note that the plural is now in common usage.

When a man or woman performing a sexual act gets so far into the experience that their tubes go into an involuntary series of minor muscular spasms, the brain follows up with a sensation anywhere from OK to exsanguinated and the whole package is called

orgasm. When you consider the amount of effort employed in understanding why people feel depressed, it comes as some surprise that nobody has yet fathomed the orgasm. The best that the neuroscientists can come up with is the rather limp statement that some aspects of it resemble the sneeze.

Male orgasm is almost invariably accompanied by ejaculation. The orgasm varies in intensity but probably not in type. Female orgasms are said to come in many different patterns and to consist of three distinct types – the clitoral (small fun), the vaginal (big fun) and the multiple (ring me next week).

Sperm
Sperm is the male seed. Each spermatozoon resembles a microscopic tadpole. The average male ejaculate is 3 mls, or one heaped teaspoonful, and contains 300 million of the things. The United Kingdom's gross national product is 540,000,000,000,000,000 sperms per annum.

Sperms swim at the rate of 18cm (7 inches) per hour and so would take 2,500 years to cross from New York to Penzance, if their average life expectancy were not limited to a long weekend.

Fertilisation
The buck-shot approach of the male seed-planter may appear to be wasteful but is necessitated by the awful inefficiency of the human reproductive tract. Any sperm making the distance is a hero of Herculean attributes.

To get past the cervix, climb up the uterine wall and find a Fallopian tube it must be armed with the physiological equivalent of an oxyacetylene torch, a set of Alpine crampons, several large-scale Ordinance Survey maps and a gold American Express card. Once there, the chances of meeting a willing egg coming in the opposite direction, in the dark, are only around 1 per cent.

Even if **fertilisation** is successful it is estimated that one in every three embryos are naturally miscarried within the first two weeks of 'pregnancy' without the mother being any the wiser.

Erogenous Zones

Both men and women are blessed with parts of their superficial anatomy which are more sensitive than other bits to stroking, licking and other interesting gestures. These are referred to as **erogenous zones**. Not surprisingly they lie in places where you are not likely to be touched during the course of a normal day's work.

Maps of the erogenous zones are available from most disreputable bookshops. We suggest you ignore them and go rambling on your own over each new pasture that comes your way. Partners vary.

Ear lobes, breasts, necks and anywhere within six inches of the sexual apparati are usually good bets. Navels, backs of knees and tips of toes (once boots are removed) are longshots but can be astoundingly effective.

G Spots are the invention of American magazines for feisty spinsters. The ultimate G Spot is the part of the anatomy which when delicately prodded will reduce its owner to a megasensual jelly. Theories regarding its location suggest that it lies somewhere unspeakably rude and that the process of finding it will be pretty arousing in itself.

Orientation

Most gays recognise their orientation at or soon after puberty. The simplest way to tell is to examine your fantasies. If they are exclusively gay then so are you.

Psychoanalysts and tortured souls tend to attribute male homosexuality to dominant mothers, ineffectual fathers and fear of having a tiny plonker.

In reality, though gays may become neurotic as a result of being clandestine and dishonest, or else by being honest and discriminated against, most start out as well-adjusted as any other spotty adolescent.

4 per cent of men and 2–3 per cent of women are exclusively or nearly exclusively homosexual. Another 10 per cent will have a homosexual experience at some time. A further 10 per cent are bisexual, which as Woody Allen pointed out doubles the chance of a good night out on Saturdays.

Level of Activity

The philosopher Emmanuel Kant died aged eighty, unperturbed by the fact that his virgo was still intacta. While sexual inactivity can be a front for unacknowledged homosexuality, a few people simply do not possess a sex drive. For them, **asexuality** is a normal state of affairs (or rather lack of them).

At the opposite extreme reliable research has found rare examples of sexually contented individuals who have it away three times a day for decades.

Men reach a peak of activity in their teens but, as they keep assuring themselves, make technical improvements well into middle age. Women reach both maximum revs and smoothest technique in their fourth decade. Unfortunately they are tilted off course by the **menopause** which has an effect on performance rather like that of an albatross being tapped on the beak by a DC 10.

Social Factors
'Society', the faceless ogre blamed by sociologists for all our ills, does not fit us for realistic relationships. Growing up, getting married, having two beautiful children and living happily ever after rarely, if ever, happens. In real life:

- one third of British brides are pregnant
- two thirds of teenage marriages fail within five years
- one in five children do not have the parents they think they have and
- 40 per cent of married people have had an extra-marital affair.

Contraception

Contraceptive methods demonstrate homo sapiens at his most outrageously inventive. Before the biotechnologically cool 'birth control pill' was invented, all contraceptives were based on putting something in the way of nature's intention.

Placing something unpleasant between you and your partner was called **'barrier' contraception.** *Doing* something unpleasant was called **'natural' contraception.** We will deal with this latter form of potty practice first.

Coitus Interruptus
Also known as the Withdrawal Method, or in the Cornish vernacular 'Getting off at Launceston Station

instead of carryin' on to Plymouth Central.'

In the Bible, this was the method employed by Onan who 'spilt his seed on the ground' when having it away with his sister-in-law. Unfortunately God was not impressed by his consideration and struck him dead.

Whilst disaster of that sort is uncommon nowadays, act of God may intervene in another way. Accidental pregnancy occurs at the rate of 7 per cent per annum in regular performers.

The advantages are that it is free, does not require a trip to the doctor and cannot be left in the hotel room whilst you are down at the beach.

Rhythm Method
Involves collecting vaginal secretion and examining it to see if it has the consistency of egg-white.

Serious protagonists also take their body temperature every day and knock off sexual activity when they heat up by a part of a degree. You might say that to label either of the above procedures 'natural' is a misuse of English, but so it goes. With a failure rate of 15 per cent a year this method is not recommended to those who wish to stay childless or to piano teachers.

The Sheath
We are supposed to believe that the contraceptive sheath was invented by Dr. Condom, court physician to King Charles II. The aim was to save His Majesty from the ravages of syphilis and it was only when he was investigated for infertility that its contraceptive potential was recognised.

The original sheaths were made from stretched sheeps' intestines. Modern versions are moulded in transparently thin vulcanised rubber, ribbed for sensitivity and available in more colours than a Rolls Royce.

Some sport strange nobbles for extra stimulation though for whom is unclear. The failure rate is 3 per cent per annum for careful couples.

The Diaphragm
Also known as 'the cap', this female rejoinder to the sheath originates in the Middle Ages when prostitutes in continental Europe started using half lemons as contraceptive devices. The three-fold principle was that the juice acted as a spermicide, the inverted lemon wrapped itself around the cervix as a physical barrier and the citrus aroma was more attractive to the customer. We do not recommend this method as we imagine it would sting like fury. Oranges might be kinder. Pineapples are to be avoided.

The modern rubber version orginates from late 19th century Amsterdam, hence the name 'Dutch Cap'. It has a 12 per cent per annum failure rate.

The Sponge
To fathom the minds of the inventors of the condom and diaphragm is not too difficult. In considering the contraceptive **sponge** it is possible that we are dealing with a personality in crisis.

Popular in the United States, these disposable polyurethane pads are impregnated with a spermicidal cream which only works if it is lathered. The principle is that the woman wets the pad, works it into a foam and then inserts it to cover the cervix. So, if you know where your cervix is and can hit it first time with a slimy, soapy bodge of goo at a time when you probably have your mind on something much more exciting, then this is the method for you. To add to the fun, the regular user failure rate is 17 per cent per annum.

Spermicides

Users of barrier contraceptives who wish to improve safety standards will use a dash of cream, gel or foam.

The original materials used by South American Indians included pulped cactus, though it is not recorded whether the primary effect was by spermicidal action or spiking the invader. The Ancient Egyptians are believed to have used pessaries made from a paste of honey and warm crocodile dung. Macerated wolf's testis and oil-soaked wool were popular ingredients in Eastern Europe.

The Coil

Nobody is quite sure how these objects work or why the odd squiggly copper-lined plastic wires used nowadays are so effective as contraceptives. There are sixty million women walking around today with an alien object in their uterus and forty million of them are Chinese, which must mean something.

The Arabs have been 'protecting' their camels with stones for several thousand years. The dual principle is that a stone in the camel's cervix stops pregnancy and a couple of unfriendly rocks lower down blunts the ardour of any randy young buck camel trying the hump too often.

2,500 years ago in Kos, **Hippocrates** used ivory, ebony, platinum and diamond on his private patients and glass beads for his NHS work.

Casanova carried a pouch of gold marbles with which, ultimately, to protect some of his ladies. Hence confusing literary references to his Golden Balls.

The disadvantages of this method are that they can be painful to fit and sometimes get infected. The advantages are that they have a failure rate as low as

1.4 per cent per annum and that you can get on with the matter in hand without having to stop and grope for something else.

The Pill
Every year 30,000 million contraceptive pills are eaten worldwide. If the Pope freed the third world from perpetual fertility then that number might double.

When the history of the 20th century is written by our great grandchildren, Marx and Hitler may warrant a couple of paragraphs apiece but **Dr. Pincus** and his Pill will have a chapter all to themselves. Nowadays there are half a dozen different hormone cocktails available.

The most acceptable attitude to adopt is to raise moral dilemmas about fertility control, question the long-term effects on health, castigate male-dominated scientific medicine for the pill's essentially Chauvinistic social role and make damn sure that you or your partner is on it.

Modern pills contain miniscule amounts of hormone which are just enough to con the body into thinking it is slightly pregnant and so need not bother to produce eggs. The potential health damaging effects of (unwanted) pregnancy are far greater than the pill-related risks implied in recent, badly-designed research projects. A three-monthly injectable version sometimes assists the forgetful. Failure rates are as low as 0.2 per cent per annum.

The Mexicans found out centuries ago that Dioscorea, the wild yam vine, had both contraceptive and abortive properties. The first commercial versions of 'the pill' were derived from the plant but the profits went to the U.S.A.

The only attempt to market a male pill in recent years was brought to a halt by the unfortunate side effect of turning the eyeballs pink. Perhaps researchers should investigate the claims of **Aetios**, the Greek apothecary of the 6th century B.C. who temporarily sterilised men by having them drink an infusion of willow bark laced with flambéed mule testicles.

Sterilisation
The final cut.

In women the operation involves fastening a clip across each Fallopian tube via a tiny incision in the abdomen. In men the tubes are actually snipped by the surgeon (**vasectomy**). Some female operations can be reversed but if you try to replumb the sterilised man it probably won't make a vas deferens.

In the early 1970s doctors in New York devised a miniature, gold three-way tube to be inserted into the vas at the time of ectomy. They claimed it offered the chance of reconnection at a later date. Its inventor called it a 'phaser', the marketing chaps dubbed it 'the Golden Tap' and the English labelled it a 'stopcock'. Nothing has been seen of it since.

Alternative Contraception
In ancient China, women were persuaded to drink twenty-four tadpoles in the Spring to avoid pregnancy throughout the summer. If this failed then the following year they were advised to eat bees.

The modern Chinese possess a substance called **gossypol**. Having established that men working in the cotton-seed oil business were finding great difficulty in siring children, Chinese scientists isolated a chemical

21

from the oil which guarantees to make any man subfertile. Unfortunately it also takes his ardour away and causes physical debilitation to a pre-pubertal state. American hormonal experts call it the 'Chinese Take-Away'.

Diseases

The least erotic aspects of sexual activity are microscopic. If you are prone to indecision and so experiment with a number of sexual partners, you will eventually encounter one of the creatures which reach the parts most lagers merely nullify.

Ancient diseases have Latin names to make them sound more respectable. Treponema pallidum (pox), Neisseria gonorrhoea (clap), Pediculosis pubis (crabs) and Herpes genitalis (herpes) are just a few of the friends of the promiscuous or plain unlucky.

Modern epidemics are given initials by frightened scientists. Non-Specific Urethritis (NSU) is quietly inflaming large numbers of female pelvises throughout the Western World and rendering a sizeable proportion of sufferers incapable of motherhood. Acquired Immune Deficiency Syndrome (AIDS) is so horrid that it could have been invented by the Spanish Inquisition.

The first attempt to stamp out venereal disease was in 3,000 B.C. After lamping the Medianites the Israelites took advantage of the more shapely spoils of war. Within days, Moses records that '. . . there was a plague against the congregation of the Lord', so the holy prophet ordered that all Medianite women who had 'known man by lying with him' should be summarily slaughtered. 24,000 corpses later, the epidemic was controlled.

Gonorrhoea

'The perilous infirmity of burning' was recorded as early as the 12th century in London brothels. The French, ever a blunt breed, preferred the term 'La pisse chaude'. It accounts for 50,000 new victims each year in the U.K. Until recently, the mearest whiff of penicillin was enough to make the bugs commit mass suicide; some modern gonococci are made of sterner stuff.

Syphilis

Pox is rare nowadays, only 2,000 or so new cases cropping up each year in the U.K. A big spot (chancre) on or near the obvious places qualifies the bearer for membership of an elite victims' association boasting amongst its past members: Abraham, Bathsheba, Catherine the Great, Charlemagne, Cleopatra, Christopher Columbus, Goya, Henry VIII, Herod (whose private parts were 'putrified and eaten by worms'), Julius Caesar, Keats, Mussolini, Napoleon, Samson (and Delilah), Schubert, Van Gogh and even good King Wenceslas.

The main drawback of syphilis is that if it is not treated it waits around in the body for a decade or two often driving its owner-occupier insane, before bringing about an unpleasant demise.

When it was rife in 16th century Europe the British called it the French disease, the French called it the Italian disease, the Italians called it the Spanish disease and the Spanish declared war on the British. When the Japanese introduced it to China they called it 'Manka bassam' – the Portuguese disease.

Herpes

Genital herpes is caused by the same viruses as cold sores on the lips and experts are in no doubt that the fashion for oral sex is responsible for the current popularity of this infection.

If you catch herpes then the chances are that you have a friend for life. All is not gloom and despondency though. Like any good friend herpes only shows up occasionally, usually at inconvenient moments and with decreasing frequency as you get older.

NSU

This affects as many as 130,000 people each year in Britain alone. Until recently it was also know as GOK (God Only Knows) as the bug which caused it was not identified. It turns out that the offending organism is a beast called Chlamydia trachomatis, an unholy alliance of bacterium and virus.

The bad news is that it can go for months without showing its presence and can, in the meantime, render you infertile (sometimes forever). The good news is that it is easily annihilated with tetracycline drugs.

Trichomonas

A peculiar item which naturally inhabits the vagina in one British woman in five without causing much fuss. If it starts breeding copiously however, it develops into an infection which can be passed on to others by guess what sort of activity. Of all the varities of sexually transmission disease it is the only one which can definitely be caught from lavatory seats.

Condylomata

The fancy name for warts. All warts are caused by

viruses and can be passed on sexually, especially if they are located on or near the relevant organs. Practitioners of alternative medicine were dismayed when a properly controlled scientific study showed that using witchcraft to charm the things away was no more effective than leaving well alone. However, they rallied when it was found that the wart-bashing wonder-drug podophyllin was in fact no more than extract of mandrake root.

If you need to communicate to unwanted guests at a boring dinner party that it is time for them to go, you might like to render a description of the most evil and ugliest of genital warts from any good medical textbook. Look under Buschke-Lowenstein Giant Condyloimata, preferrably on a full stomach.

Crabs

If the above diseases represent the flora of the nether regions then pediculosis pubis is the fauna. Wee jumping creatures in the genital hedgerow should not be made the subject of a conservation order.

AIDS

AIDS is not funny, not yet curable and not likely to go away. It is spread by HIV, a virus with more disguises that Micky Spillane but less subtle in its lethality.

Anyone who has ever had sex with another person can theoretically be a carrier, but if you treat every new acquaintance as a potential source of disease you will go barmy long before you risk catching it. High risk groups are promiscuous gay or bisexual men, prostitutes, drug abusers who inject, and anyone who cannot remember whose bed it is.

SEX AROUND THE WORLD

Sex happens everywhere. From the most opulent ecosystems of West coast America to the war-torn, famine-stricken plains of East Africa people find the time, space and energy to indulge in their version of love making. What is astounding is the number of quaint and peculiar practices which survive and flourish in foreign parts.

Mutilation

One of the things which sets the British apart from less reserved peoples is our unwillingness to redesign our anatomy.

In Thailand men have taken to inserting plastic beads under the skin of their penises with the object of giving their partners better vibrations. So convinced are they of the efficacy of the technique that they will perform the procedure themselves without using any anaesthetic.

Circumcision – peeling bits away from penises – has been going on for thousands of years. It is said to reduce the risk of infection. Australian aborigines go one step further by actually splitting the tip of the penis so that it resembles the two-headed organ of a kangaroo. The poor Ponpeans of the Caroline Islands not only have the underside of their penis slit but also lose one testis at the same time.

Female circumcision is usually part of a religious rite. The East African version involves trimming away part of the vaginal lips and in the Middle East it may also involve removing the clitoris, the idea being to deny the women sexual pleasure and thus render her faithful.

The religious rites of American women involve breasts. **Mammoplasty**, the medical word for cutting breasts down to size, is the third commonest non-essential operation in the U.S.A. It is surpassed in popularity only by rhinoplasty (a nose job) and breast enhancement, the implantation of floppy bags of silica.

Such vanity cuts no ice with the Mbuti pygmies, destined by genetic endowment to be short in stature but plentiful of thoracic fat. Their womenfolk simply sling the excess over their shoulders.

Education

Modern British schools teach **sex education** which is surprisingly realistic and almost informative. The same cannot be said of many foreign equivalents.

The worst deal for males must be among the Sambians of Melanesia. They teach the younger lads to fellate the older lads so as to achieve manhood.

The exposure of children to first hand experience of sex is frowned upon in most Western cultures as it is associated with child abuse and exploitation by adults. The Lepcha of the Himalayas, however, actually *show* their children how to make love and teach them methods of foreplay. Further South on the Indian sub-continent the Muria build sacred compounds called Ghotuls in which pre-pubertal children are encouraged to learn about sexual acts. **Virginity** is lost by the age of six. In southern central Africa, the Chewa assist their daughters in finding suitable husbands by building huts outside the village for sexual liaisons and exploratory play. A similar attitude is adopted by the Ifugoros of the Philippines who encourage their unmarried but sexually active youths to share mixed sex dormitory accommodation and test all the options until they find a suitable match.

Virginity and its surrender is subject to many a cultural quirk. Many African witch doctors carry with them a greasy pole called the 'marriage stick', for deflowering purposes. The Kurds of North East Iran like to see a blood-stained wedding sheet on the morning after a marriage ceremony as proof of both consumation and pre-marital purity. In some Somali tribes the bride and groom are expected to take time out from the ceremony to perform in the privacy of a wedding hut while the village elders hold silent vigil outside. Some conservative cultures in the Far East and around the Turkish end of the Mediterranean are so obsessional about deflowering that a spinster who has 'lapsed' will often have a small operation to restitch her hymen in order to remain marriageable.

Habits

Surprisingly, no authoritative text exists on the international variations in sexual tastes or techniques. 'Around the World in 80 Lays' is a guaranteed best seller waiting for a research team. There are however many indications that attitudes to sexual practices vary widely from culture to culture.

Even something as innocuous as the **kiss** is not universally popular. The Eskimos rub noses for fear of chapped lips, the Kwakiutl Indians suck each other's tongues and the Sirionos of South America appear to lack any intermediate show of affection between wishing each other 'Good evening' and the commencement of rutting.

The French kiss was invented by the inhabitants of Pays de Mont, a small town in Britanny, who had concluded that their town was becoming overpopulated. They did not fancy moving out and had no money to build new housing so, with a great sense of communal sacrifice they agreed to stop procreating for a few years. They substituted for their absent pleasures by exploring the possibilities of the oral safari, to the delight of toothpaste manufacturers ever since.

Masturbation is an international pastime but the only group which positively approves the practice in married women is the East African muslim community. Their logic is that only a superhuman man can cater to the sexual and emotional needs of the average woman and so it is perfectly healthy for her to lend a hand, as it were. The only recorded Western equivalent dates from the Napoleonic wars when French soldiers would give their loved one a dildo to tide her over until they returned from battle.

Lecherous males might wish they had been born into the Thonga, an African tribe who believe that a man should have as many wives as he is capable of servicing in a single heavy session. Equally sexist is the arrangement among Comanche Indians that the sisters of a heavily pregnant woman should see to the needs of her husband while she is indisposed.

India and Nepal boast dozens of examples of Hindu temples, the outside walls of which are covered in carvings of copulating crowds. The implication is that there was once, and may still be, a cultural recognition that in the right circumstances oral, anal and group sex, preferably with unrestrained orgasm, are jolly good things.

Muslim attitudes are confusing to the Western mind. On the one hand the yashmak-and-all-over-maxi-skirt tends to imply cultural sexophobia. On the other, Arabic erotic art and literature has a long and relatively respectable pedigree. Polygamy too is ill understood by Europeans. The simplest explanation is that any group constantly at war with someone or other for the greater glory of God is likely to be suffering a shortage of intact marriageable males.

Beliefs

The Victorian moralists are not the only example of a group of sexual crazies. Muslims and Orthodox Jews still harbour a belief that a menstruating woman is 'unclean'. Buddhist temples in Indonesia go along with this view and often employ specially trained sniffer dogs to keep such she-devils out of the sacred portals.

The Thais believe that the size of a man's nose is indicative of the size of his penis. The Japanese hold similar views on the relationship between lips and vaginae, which might explain their preference for making no comment.

Several examples exist of African tribes who believe matrimony to be ill-advised between partners whose genitalia are not of compatible proportions. The introduction to the in-laws – a tricky moment in any culture – is enlivened by the necessity for them to inspect and pronounce upon the acceptability of the spare parts deal before agreeing to the purchase.

The border between bizarre belief and frank delusion is most difficult to define in the field of **aphrodisiacs**. Since the dawn of time the human race, usually in its male incarnation, has been searching for substances to enhance sexual performance.

Relatively sensible ideas have included potions

based on weak alcohol, ginseng, cannabis or opium – though this last substance has the unfortunate side-effects of addiction, bankruptcy, debilitation, eventual impotence and premature death. Symbolic substances have included ground rhino horn or deer antler (for hard-horned erections), olives (for firm testes), oysters (for luscious labia), okra (for better lubrication) and peppers (for heating up the action). Regrettably the list does not end here.

The Chinese have always been exponents of lateral thinking. It was their ancestors who first suggested imbibing semen or menstrual blood for its invigorating qualities. Both were said to be more potent if used as the moistening agent for dried eagle droppings. The fresh placenta, eaten raw or stir-fried was said to ensure the rapid return of the mother's libido. Warm deer's blood had its supporters, as did the macerated testes of freshly slaughtered cattle. Gourmets professed a preference for human tissues and pointed out that these commodities could be found on the corpses of enemies in battle. Undoubtedly the sickest and possibly the saddest was the belief among eunuchs of the Chinese Imperial court that their untimely ripped parts would regrow if they feasted on the still-warm brains of recently decapitated criminals. Compared to the above, the old West African staple of dried fruit bat seems positively palatable.

Our advice is that the only effective aphrodisiac is celery. You don't eat it, you use it as a splint.

SEX MANUALS

For as long as mankind has been doing it, someone somewhere has known how to do it better. This is as true of sex as it is of gardening. Sex manuals have been around for 4,500 years but we still have not learnt enough to make them unnecessary. This is because most are terribly disappointing.

The Original
The Yellow Emperor, **Huang Ti**, commissioned the first one in 2600 B.C. It described techniques for kissing, titillating the erogenous zones and timing the pelvic thrust to maximum effect. It instructed that a healthy sex life increased one's life expectancy.

Its contents were advanced for the time and its marketing was inspired. The 'facts' were presented in the form of a series of conversations between the Emperor and three fantasy women. Su Nu, the Plain Girl, was the clean, homely type. The Elected Girl was a flirt who rarely delivered the goods. The Dark Girl was the technical expert who taught the Emperor – and thereby the reader – all manner of sexual tricks. Not surprisingly, it became cult reading and was a most respectable gift at a wedding.

The Jade Room
The most prolific sex manual compilers were the scribes of the Han Dynasty in the first three centuries A.D. Their best sellers were *Su Nu Ching* (Lady Purity's Manual), *Yu Fang Mi Chueh* (Secrets of the Jade Room), and *Yu Fang Chiu Yau* (The Jade Room Guide). Amateurs often think that the Jade Room was a high-class Imperial brothel. A bluffer will know that in fact it was highly respectable slang for the vagina.

Kama Sutra

Vatsyayana, the 4th century Brahmin priest who compiled the *Kama Sutra* would turn in his grate (he was cremated) if he could see what modern man has done to his encyclopaedia.

He barely indulged in sexual practice himself. In fact the Kama Sutra was the equivalent of *Mrs. Beeton's Book of Household Management*, a sort of yuppies' handbook for 1,000 years' worth of Indian social climbers. Sexual hints are included but they make up only a part of the central section of the book. Recipes for love potions appear but so do cures for spots. How to please your sexual partner is on a par with how to wire a plug.

What gave it a reputation as a dirty book fit for a king were perhaps the articles on how to enlarge your sexual organs and what the Brahmin-about-town wears on his private parts. Its few dozen illustrated suggestions for acrobatic love-making are not drawn to scale. If they had been, their impossibility would be obvious. Any man attempting the famous 'Bull among Cows' is likely to develop terminal lumbago.

The Art of Love

Ting Hsuan, the 7th century Chinese writer, was the first of many authors to say 'art' when he meant 'types' and 'love' when he meant 'sex'. In fact he had a way with words generally. Among the names he gives to the vagina are the 'Deep Vale', the 'Open Peony' and the 'Chicken's Tongue'. The male organ is referred to as the 'Turtle Head', the 'Swelling Mushroom' and the 'Positive Peak'.

The Art of Love illustrates 30 poses for keen contortionists and gives them wonderfully descriptive names, such as 'Unicorn's Horn', 'Galloping Steed', 'Jumping White Tiger' and the excruciating 'Flying Ducks Reversed'.

Priceless Recipes
Sun Szumo was a Chinese court physician of the 9th century. His leaning was towards the philosophy of sexual practice and he was exceedingly smart. This is the chap to quote at dinner parties as none of your fellow guests will have heard of him.

Sun Szumo held that after the age of 40, a man's potency declined and so he should learn advanced sexual technique whilst in his mid-thirties. He believed that before that age a man was too ignorant, and after it too feeble, to understand what he was doing.

The Science of Coition
Lesser known, and deservedly so, is **Jalal al Din al Siyuti**, the Arab theologist who perhaps expressed Islamic thinking better in his book *An Exposition of the Science of Coition*. This was the first compendium of marital arts from the Middle East. It was also the first text in which the woman is seen clearly as a passive object in a ritual which barely concerns her. Its opening lines are:

'Praise to the Lord who . . . made the thighs of women anvils for the spear handles of men.'

The Perfumed Garden
The original *Perfumed Garden for the Soul's Delectation* was written by a Tunisian Sheikh called **Al Nafwazi** in the 16th century. It had an Islamic ring to it but lacked the chauvinistic approach of Jalal al

Din. It opened with the far more equitable words:

'Praise to the Lord who ... destined the natural parts of man to afford the greatest enjoyment to women.'

It is hailed as an erotic masterpiece but is useful too. It includes a Good Woman Guide, outlining the sort of attributes a man should look out for in a potential conquest and a Good Man Guide, detailing both the standard fittings and deluxe items available in a decent male.

Psychology of Sex
Havelock Ellis is the grand-daddy of modern sexology. His first attempt at *Studies in the Psychology of Sex* was published in the United States in 1896, and was periodically updated over the next 30 years. He had theories on just about everything which was fine because at that time practically nobody else had.

Potential students should be warned however that as well as being innovative, thought-provoking and decades ahead of its time, *Studies* is monumentally dull. You are not advised to read it in bed unless you have difficulty sleeping.

Sexual Behaviour
In 1948, **Alfred Kinsey** shocked middle America with the publication of *Sexual Behaviour in the Human Male*. It was all about the practices of his fellow Americans. He followed up in 1953 with a volume on the human female.

By trade Kinsey was a zoologist and his real interest in life was the gall wasp. He collected 3,000,000 of the things and produced the definitive work on sub-species in the gall wasp world.

Applying the same method to the examination of

several thousand sexual histories, he concluded over the years that 4 per cent of men and 2 per cent of women are exclusively homosexual and that 6 per cent of men are homosexual for a significant part of their adolescence. He was the first person to state that 98 per cent of men and over 50 per cent of women masturbate. He also re-invented the multiple orgasm, but only for women.

Human Sexual Response

'The Reproduction Biology Research Project' is the name of the work carried out by **William Masters** and **Virginia Johnson** at the Washington University in St. Louis. The most famous book they produced from it was *Human Sexual Response*, which saw the light of day in April 1966.

Between 1960 and 1965 they watched what happens when a sexually mature man or woman enjoys sex. 382 anonymous women and 312 anonymous men masturbated or had sexual intercourse a total of 10,000 times under laboratory conditions, i.e. in front of the team of wholly disinterested professionals. Insofar as anyone choosing to get laid in a laboratory is 'normal', these measurements have for over twenty years defined the averages and the outer limits of normal sexual experience.

Findings include the fact that men ejaculate between 3 and 7 times during orgasm at a rate of 1.25 times per second and that women can have up to 12 contractions during orgasm with some able to manage an instant repeat. The record was 25 contractions in 43 seconds. The clitoris is back in position within 10 seconds of completing an orgasm, the vagina returns to its normal state within 15 minutes but the cervix remains gaping slightly for 30 minutes.

Many of their findings were the result of a novel technique in which a see-through imitation penis, individually tailored to the requirements of the female participant was inserted into her Jade Room and manipulated in realistically rhythmic fashion. This enabled cameras and fibroscopes to see and measure exactly what was happening.

No doubt their shared experiences contributed to the fact that Mrs Johnson later became Mrs Masters.

The Hite Report

Shere Hite may sound like a penis enlargement cream but in fact is an American journalist who reached fame and fortune by interviewing women who answered a magazine advertisement, about their sex lives. *The Hite Report* was a sort of vox pop Kinsey with a Cosmopolitan bias. If you hear someone stating with confidence that 39 per cent of all women under 35 feature Barry Manilow's nose in their masturbatory fantasies then the information might well have come from Hite. It is worth knowing that in 1981 Ms Hite did a similar study on men.

Good reads for a long train journey in a deserted railway carriage.

Joy of Sex

The Joy of Sex is the million copy best-seller of the modern sex manuals. **Alex Comfort**, its author, is a cuddly old man who writes simply and sympathetically about the troubles we mortals find in keeping sex scintillating. The early Chinese would not be impressed by its absence of soul but as a book for its time, it reflects perfectly the 'suck-it-and-see' approach of the 20th century sexual practitioner.

SEXUAL HEROES

The accolade of great lover is attributed to few. Those who have attained the title appear to have had four things in common:

1. The ability to give graphic descriptions of their own sexual prowess.
2. An unconscionably ugly face or body.
3. A capacity for romance which matches that of an 'A' level Biology course.
4. A chance acquaintance with an otherwise unoccupied author or publisher willing to tell all abroad.

As in any other field of endeavour, those who are not born of high rank are more likely to make the big time if they sleep with someone famous.

It is important to carry with you the case vignettes of a few adept practitioners but we advise caution. When relating their exploits you should temper each one with a healthy measure of disbelief. Our selection consists of some of the more reliable histories.

King David & King Solomon
The Old Testament translators used some splendid euphemisms when speaking of sex. To 'lie with' and to 'know' may be translated into modern vernacular as to have' and to 'give one to'.

King David had eight wives and ten concubines. Only when well past pensionable age, did he suffer a sudden loss of power and his loins 'gat no heat'. Because he was the King the elders shied away from putting him in the county asylum and instead sent for a virgin, called Abishag. Alas, even she could not tempt his fire and he died soon after.

Solomon had a one track mind. He specialised in

dowries. By the time of his death he is said to have had 700 wives in addition to his 300 concubines. This is not to be believed as the use of random high numbers was common in ancient scriptures and denotes merely 'quite a lot'.

There was a streak of gourmet in him. He tried to acquire at least one princess from every state in the known world, including Egypt, his favourite being the Queen of Sheba. You might care to suggest, should anyone ask what made her so special, that she was the only one whose name he could remember.

Chou Hsin and Yang Ti

Chou Hsin was a playboy king of the Shang dynasty, who lived around 1,500 B.C. He was said regularly to entertain ten partners in one session and to have invented his own 'position', involving strutting around the room with an impaled woman entwined around his waist. Unfortunately the authenticity of this tale is not improved by the additional 'facts' that he was over 8 feet tall and could kill tigers and leopards with his bare hands.

More likely are the accounts of the behaviour of Yang Ti, Emperor of the Sui Dynasty in the 7th century A.D. He had one Queen, two Deputy Queens, 6 official consorts, 72 royal occasionals and a palace staff of 3,000 handmaidens who would, but only if asked. The quaint part of his reputation was his idea of a good picnic. If ever he went journeying around his Empire he ensured that amongst the caravan were ten carts each accommodating a naked maiden draped on a red satin sheet like a prawn on a smoked salmon canapé.

Messalina

Valeria Messalina was the wife of Emperor Claudius. She married him when she was 16 but already an established man-eater. A typical story of her antics stemmed from a time when Claudius was away on business (the 2,000 year old excuse). She was left both miffed and unsated, so challenged a well known Roman whore to a man contest. Each lady tried to knock off more coconuts in one session than her opponent, the winner being awarded their combined fees. Messalina won by servicing over 50 prominent Roman citizens before her hips gave way. Psychologists later tried to immortalise her exploits by giving nymphomania the homonym of the 'Messalina Complex'. She died at 30, probably of old age.

Cleopatra

Apart from bathing in asses' milk and hailing a variety of Caesars, Queen Cleopatra's greatest claim to fame was as the ancient world's finest fellatrice. She was reported once to have performed her art on 100 Roman soldiers in one evening. We take it she was a sucker for any man in uniform. Her name in Greek is Merichane which is held to mean 'she who gapes wide for ten thousand'.

Casanova

The most famous of the Great Lovers was born in Venice in 1725. His name was Jacques Casanova, or in English, Jake Newhouse, and according to a contemporary 'He would have been handsome, had he not been very ugly.'

He started young, being expelled from a seminary at the age of 16 for immoral conduct.

His style was that of a collector. For him a woman's most attractive feature was not her virtue but her co-operation in his essentially selfish quest to try sex in all its forms. The acts he remembered were those with the youngest, oldest, tallest, shortest, fattest, most disfigured and most famous of his co-workers. He could recall details like the number of chairs employed in the performance, the public park involved and the position of the lady's left foot at the moment of orgasm. It was the faces and surnames which eluded him.

Comfort yourself with the fact that after he turned 40, his reputation sank to that of languid bore and most of his later sexual adventures had to be purchased. He was 73 when he died. Rumours that the cause of death was syphilis are merely the conjecture of envious lesser mortals.

Catherine the Great

Born four years after Casanova, it is sad to think that the woman correctly addressed as 'Empress Ekaterina of all the Russias' never met him. They would have made a lovely couple.

She was married at the age of 16 to Peter, the young Russian emperor, who was a terrible disappointment. His inability to sire an heir led to the interference of his mother, the Empress Elizabeth. First she paid a courtier called Saltikov to seduce Catherine, then had the resulting child whisked away at birth and banned her from further dalliance. The young woman spent the rest of her life in rebellion.

She was not naturally attractive. She used her position to entrap men, gaining a reputation for elevating her conquests and ruining those who snubbed her. She chose only handsome men and made

Herculean demands of them.

She clearly distinguished between 'lovers' to whom she remained surprisingly constant and 'session players' whose role was that of a human dildo.

Each stud was first examined for venereal disease by the Court Physician and then tested by her éprouveuse, a trusted lady-in-waiting who assessed the new lover's skills. If he was passed fit he was allowed a stab at entertaining the Empress.

Her more outlandish biographers claim that she died at the age of 67 in the act of copulation with a stallion harnessed above her bed. In fact she died of a heart attack at her desk, in her office, though she would no doubt have preferred the alternative version.

The Also-Rans

The most distinguished sexual autobiography is *My Life and Loves* by **Frank Harris**. He was a journalist and so his tall tales of ribald fun are probably no more accurate than a newspaper editorial. However, as it is well known that a proportion of journalists will hump anything which is still breathing, one cannot be sure.

The other character whose existence is questionable is **Walter**, 'the English Casanova', whose interesting adventures are chronicled by Kronhausen. The text is not easy to find and so we suggest that you limit any comments about Walter to a stark disbelief in his existence.

But there is no doubt about **Mrs Feodor Vassilet** (1708–1782), the most prolific child bearer of all time. She produced 16 pairs of twins, 7 sets of triplets and 4 sets of quadruplets, a total of 69 children, all but two of whom reached adulthood.

SEX AND THE LAW

English sex law is based on a mixture of confused morality and obscure precedents. The absence of a national philosophy of sex leads inevitably to a situation in which the law is powerless on the one hand whilst oppressive on the other. You will find little difficulty persuading friends that they have all had unlawful sexual relations at some time, a line of conversation particularly useful when trying to stir up stuffy relatives.

Gender Bending

In law you are born either male or female and are stuck with that sex until death. This may not sound particularly stupid until one considers the half per cent of the population who by dint of genetic or developmental blunder are neither one nor the other: sufferers from Kleinfelter's or Turner's syndrome, for example, whose chromosomes, like their sexual anatomy, do not fit the genetic norm.

The extreme idiocy of this law is seen when a baby who is genetically male suffers a hormonal accident in the womb and comes out looking female. Even if subsequent treatment rectifies the situation, the bearded second row forward will still be a girl in law. He will not be conscripted at time of war, admitted to the main pavilion at Lords or allowed to marry a woman.

Age of Consent

The age at which a female can give valid consent to sexual intimacy is sixteen. For males there is no limit, unless the object of their desire is another man, in which case they must be 21. Until 1929 you could have sex with a twelve year old provided she was your spouse. Prior to 1885 there was no such thing as an age of consent: Courts determined whether sex was legal by gauging whether or not children were mature enough to know what they were doing. The usual milestone was taken as twelve or fourteen years old, which was remarkable considering that in those days the average age of puberty was sixteen or seventeen.

Incest
Most adults may agree to go to bed with you unless they are close relatives. Since 1908 you have not been allowed to have sex with your parents, children, siblings or grandfather. Men are allowed a fling with granny, provided she agrees, and sex with uncles, aunts, nephews and nieces is fine provided you do not seek to wed any of them, which is a crime. Cousins are free to do as they please but halfsibs, stepfathers, stepmothers and stepchildren must keep their hands off each other.

Exhibitionism
Men cannot be the victim of a flasher. Exhibitionism is defined as 'lewdly and obscenely exposing the person to insult a female'. In practice 50 per cent of the targets are girls under sixteen but sightings are becoming less frequent.

In theory a male streaker can be arrested for indecent exposure while a female streaker is only causing a breach of the peace.

Frottage
To rub your body against a stranger in a sexually provocative way in the disco at the staff Christmas

party is considered only good manners. To do so in the queue at the staff canteen is an indecent assault punishable by up to two years in prison. The Victorians considered frotteurs to be suffering from dangerous hypersexuality and had the blighters put away in mental institutions.

Prostitution
To sell one's body for sexual purposes is not a crime. However, if you do there is no such thing as consumer protection, so beware. Neither the prostitute nor the client has any recourse to law to obtain payment or satisfaction for services.

Advertising the fact that you are open for business can be a crime in two ways. It might constitute 'soliciting' for prostitution – as can kerb-crawling. (A policeman is entitled to arrest anyone whom he reasonably suspects to be trying to attract custom, even if they are in fact waiting outside a theatre for their maiden aunt.) Or, if the prostitute is drawing attention to herself with more abandon, she may be guilty of 'riotous or indecent behaviour'.

Surprisingly as many as ten per cent of working prostitutes are men. Their status in law is the same as for women. Sex equality also holds true for brothel-keepers but not for pimps. While a man can be found guilty of living off immoral earnings, a woman in charge of a posse of prostitutes cannot. Both are liable to a charge of controlling or having influence over their employees, however, which carries a maximum sentence of seven years.

Public Places
It is illegal to make love on public monuments. Tupping at the Tate or humping on the hallowed turf

45

at Wembley is a dream which is liable to a heavy fine.

To make love in a car parked on a public right of way is indecent behaviour. If parked on private land which is out of public view it is usually considered fair sport. Special care should be taken within the precincts of Oxford and Cambridge Universities, however, as you might be liable to a fine under the Universities Act of 1825 for being 'an idle or disorderly person'.

Sodomy
Anal intercourse is the only form of coition between consenting adults which is specifically banned in English law. The only circumstances in which it may be legal is when both parties are male (see Homosexuality). The maximum penalty for a man found guilty of having anal intercourse with his wife, albeit with her full co-operation and consent, is life imprisonment.

Homosexuality
The laws governing homosexual activity may be mad but they are at least clear.

Since 1967, male homosexual activity has been legal in the U.K. provided that:

– both parties are at least 20 years and 364 days old
– both consent to the act
– neither is a serving member of Her Majesty's forces or the Merchant Navy
– nobody else is present in the room
– it is done in a private place in England or Wales which is not a toilet to which the public would have access if the participants had not locked the door.

Female homosexual activity is not and never has been illegal because Victorian legislators could not bring themselves to enlighten Her Imperial Highness when she refused to believe that such pastimes existed.

Bestiality
All sexual activities with other species are illegal. For them to be otherwise would be a gross abuse of animal rights. You should stick to eating them instead.

Necrophilia
It is illegal to have sexual relations with a dead body. Courts do not take kindly to being offered the defence that you could not tell because it did not feel any different from usual.

Marriage
The marriage contract, seen by Kant as a lease hire agreement of the procreative apparati, is not a contract for which legal redress can be sought for breaking its conditions. Penalties are not paid in fines, probation orders and custodial sentences but in terms of whether or not the injured party has the right to claim a divorce or, in some cases annulment of the marriage.

Marriages can be annulled – i.e. deemed never to have happened – if they were not presided over by an accredited person, if the two parties are closely related, if either party is under sixteen, married to someone else at the time or not of the sex they claim to be. They can be made void, which amounts to the same thing, if either party had undeclared venereal disease to which their new spouse subsequently objects or if the bride is later found to have been pregnant by another man, at the time of the wedding. If the groom has a secret bun cooking in another woman's oven then the wife has no such redress, unless she married in New Zealand of course.

Once married, the partners have a duty to do three things:
1. Consummate the relationship
2. Cultivate a mutually tolerable sex life
3. Stay faithful to each other.

Consummation means entering the penis into the vagina to a prescribed depth for a reasonable time, at least once. If you cannot or will not consummate, then your partner can appeal to have the marriage laid waste, even if you had been at it like hamsters premaritally.

A mutually tolerable sex life is hard to define. There is a case on record of a man being granted a divorce after his wife consistantly refused his 'reasonable' demand for fortnightly fun. At the opposite extreme one woman was granted freedom from the 'unreasonable' behaviour of a husband who demanded sex after every meal.

Faithfulness refers only to matters of sex but is nonetheless a tricky area. It is held to cover more than just adultery. Artificial insemination by donor without the husband's consent is out, as is an act of sexual intimacy not involving intercourse. In the right circumstances heavy petting or outrageous flirting can be held to be a breach of the marriage contract. Provocative friendships are another delight. If you make out that a Platonic friendship is really sexual in nature then this may constitute mental cruelty and Plato could be called to the witness box of the divorce court.

Living Together
Ten per cent of steady heterosexual co-habiting couples in the U.K. are not married. They may be surprised

to learn that sex between them is unlawful but relieved to know that it is not a crime. If you can fathom that then you might yet consider taking up the law. What it means is that there is a law still on the statute books which says you must not do it but there is no penalty for actually transgressing it.

Sex is only criminal between unmarried co-habiting adults if one of them is mentally defective. The solution in that case is to marry, whereafter exactly the same activities will become legal.

If a man or woman has undergone a sex change since birth then he/she may not make a heterosexual marriage as both partners, in law, will be of the same sex. A homosexual couple may not marry. However, in theory at least, a homosexual couple could marry provided that one of them was born of the opposite sex and has since had a sex change.

Attempts to make legally binding sexual contracts involving co-habitation outside marriage have no validity in English law. Be warned that if your partner deserts you twenty years after you agreed to live together unmarried, you are not entitled to 'palimoney' through a British court.

HISTORY OF SEX

Rather like yoghourt, sex has always been there but has tended to go in and out of fashion.

Many modern thinkers believe that we live in immoral (or if you prefer, 'liberated') times. This quaint idea does not bear close examination. Compared to other successful civilizations of years gone by we are sexually sensitive to the point of prudery.

Admittedly, sexual historians have their work cut out sifting the facts from a wealth of nice ideas. Most recorded information from centuries past dwells on matters of little consequence such as politics, Imperial human interest stories, invasions, massacres and that sort of thing. It is rare to find items relating to major concerns like food, booze, sex or folk-singing. To add to the difficulties, many of the accounts which do exist are hopelessly prejudiced, either due to censorship or lecherous exaggeration.

We recommend that you collect a small store of accurate information, examples of which we list below. When you hear a new story we suggest that before relating it as true, you ask yourself:

1) Could I have done it?
2) Would I have wanted to do it?
3) Would my mother have let me do it?

If the answers to (1) and (2) are 'yes' and to (3) is 'no' then quote and be damned.

Early Man

Amongst the cave paintings of the Dordogne, dating from 40,000 B.C., are several depicting early man rutting with early woman. Dirty doodling is perhaps the oldest art form on Earth, a tradition carried on to this day by the graffito artists of Inner City housing estates.

The Babylonians

These early inhabitants of Mesopotamia were the first cultural group to be branded immoral. This may have been simply the result of trial by gossip but they did produce the earliest recorded piece of erotica, a carved tablet depicting alternative copulatory poses. There is nothing subtle about this artefact but then, a civilisation which called its capital city 'Ur' was not strong on startling originality.

The Egyptians

The Egyptians invented pyramids, the aristocracy and page-boy haircuts. Lesser known but infinitely more useful creations included writing paper, poster paints and prostitutes. The earliest known fore-runners of the 'blue' media were a collection of porno hieroglyphics and 'adult-only' papyruses found in the Nile Valley. A comparison with the current output of the Color Climax Corporation of Copenhagen will show that whilst the technology has improved, the plot remains essentially the same.

The Egyptians' other claim to fame was that their royal household survived for many hundreds of years on the principle of keeping it, i.e. sex, in the family. European royalty has a tradition of marrying distant cousins but the Egyptians were far more choosy. In order of preference, the ideal child-bearer for the son of an Egyptian King was:

a) his mother
b) his sister
c) his daughter.

The Chinese

The ancient Chinese produced a greater variety of erotic objets d'art in the first millenium B.C. than any civilisation before or since. Pottery vases, statuettes, jewellery, engraved elephant tusks and even coins of the realm exist from that period, showing men and women fornicating in every conceivable position with each other, with beasts of the field and even with themselves.

The Taoists claimed at one point that immortality could be achieved by those who excelled between the sheets. This led to the Imperial court calling up legions of pretty handmaidens to assist the Emperor in his quest. It also led to Taoism gaining the approval of the court.

A few years later they suggested that young men could rise to a higher spiritual plain if they sought a deep and meaningful friendship with a heifer. Presumably, the inscrutable logic behind this was that by then there were too few handmaidens to go round.

The Greeks

In a society free from AIDS and the Moral Majority, the Athenians held that sexuality was a gift from the Gods and should be indulged as freely and wide-rangingly as felt natural.

Brothels had been known around the Eastern Mediterranean since 2,000 B.C. but the Athenians were the first to bring them under state control. The aim was to quell rowdiness and the spread of disease. The Athens Exchequer cleaned up the brothels too – for the first and last time in history, sex was subject to a purchase tax.

The Greeks brought homosexuality out of the closet. An ever practical people, they realised that a certain proportion of their population preferred partners of their own sex and that locking them away in all-male prisons was unlikely to persuade them otherwise.

The Romans

During the heyday of their Empire, the Romans had a reputation for civilised behaviour and strictish moral codes. But with the Decline and Fall, a series of ineffectual and patently unhinged Emperors gave license to evermore extreme forms of pleasure-seeking while maintaining impossibly strict legislation on the behaviour of the plebs.

Tiberius, perhaps the least hinged of the lot, being aware that it was illegal to put a virgin to death decreed that executioners rape their victims in public view prior to the killing. He was described by the official historian of the time as 'a filthy old man'.

Nero preferred larger scale spectacles. He was the Busby Berkley of orgiastic sex. A great believer in audience participation, his creations blurred the boundaries between eroticism, violence and chaos, in a way that was not questioned until 1,800 years later, by Sigmund Freud. Nero was raised by a barber and a male ballet dancer. Perhaps if he had been in analysis the history of the Western World would have been very different.

The Early Christians

Christians were the first folk in Western Europe to bring a pandemic niceness to the way they treated each other. Their idea of antisocial behaviour was to carve fishes on the wall – and let's face it, there is nothing less erotic than a fish.

The New Testament laid down a moral code which

recommended monogamous marriage and fidelity. This was a jolly sensible way of limiting sexually transmitted disease and single parent families in the days before condoms, penicillin and the DHSS.

Early Christians were permitted pre-marital sex provided it was with a view to checking out a prospective partner and not merely a means of scattering one's seed. Equally, they saw homosexuality as a bit of a waste of energy rather than a mortal sin.

Mysogeny, frigidity, homosexuality and hypocrisy were products of a later era – the Holy Roman Empire – when the Christian uprising had turned into just another revolting revolt.

The Continentals

Religion, power and sex have always been intertwined. The early Popes tended to prefer the last two.

John XII was asked to leave for turning the St John Lateran into a bordello. Leo VIII's departure was less public – he had a stroke whilst engaged in the act. Alexander VI got caught out for holding a super binge at tithe-payers' expense when he invited the prostitutes of Rome to come and dance naked in front of the Papal court. Unfortunately things got out of hand and he ended up offering prizes to the men who, in the audience's opinion, had tupped the most.

All this shenanigan was several hundred years before the Medicis and Borgias. Their specialities were incest, perversion of youth and the odd piece of gratuitous violence. The man who was recruited as candidate to heal the Great Schism which once promised to eradicate Catholicism, Balthasar Cossa, was a breath of fresh air in comparison. His memoirs revealed only the faintest smattering of close relatives, married women and Holy Sisters among his 200 conquests.

In France, the Louis dynasty were hardly bastions of propriety. Louis XIII married at 14 when he may well have been pre-pubescent. The poor lad was made to consummate the marriage the same night attended by two nurses. He was 17 before he could attempt a repeat performance. Louis XIV in addition to siring 14 heirs, formed a bevy of mistresses. He paid the better ones by granting them the income from a tobacco and meat tax imposed on the citizens of Paris. In later life he developed an anal fistula which made sex so painful that he turned to religion and château-building instead.

Louis XVI's sexual propensities helped bring about the French revolution. He had created the Palais aux Cerfs in the grounds of Versailles, where several dozen young femmes were installed for his delight at a cost to the French tax payer, in modern terms, of £750,000 per annum.

The British

In Britain neither the Ancient nor Holy Roman influence is easily discerned. Early attitudes to sex were shaped more by the Vikings and other bands of hoodlums. Virginity was retained by the fast runners.

Anglo Saxon had no word for adultery and dark age Britain had no code for morality. Chaucer's *Canterbury Tales* will attest that coupling with friends and acquaintances was seen as fair sport. It is from this era that we inherit most of the monosyllabic grunts which pass for profanities in modern English.

The Normans brought us droit du seigneur. This was the custom by which the spinsters of the Parish were allowed the privilege on the eve of their wedding to be deflowered by the lord of the manor. Feudal lords were also entitled to claim unpaid tithes from villeins in the form of sexual favours from the womenfolk. One account exists of an abbot inheriting le droit.

History books exclude the fact that when Richard the Lionheart arrived in the Holy Land on his first crusade he found that his good and faithful knights had spent all his cash on wine and women.

Surprisingly little is known about the sexual practices of the Middle Ages. The success of a good Catholic policy of monogamy and fidelity can be gauged by the fact that there was an epidemic of syphilis in the late 1400s which had the experts predicting an eradication of the race within 20 years.

It is unlikely that such concerns altered the national attitude to promiscuity, however. James I and VI was described by friends who knew him well as 'a vulgar yob who voided his full interior organs in disgusting public fashion up or down'. Either way he was the first AC/DC monarch to flaunt it; the original gay cavalier. He referred to boyfriend George Villiers, twenty-five years his junior, as 'sweet childe and wife' before making him Earl of Buckingham for his services to rhyming slang.

Pepys and other authors of the 1600s describe whoring as commonplace – just one of the options for an otherwise dull Thursday night. Good King Charles indulged openly with Nell Gwyn and enough others to sire fourteen illegitimate children – a fine testimony to Dr. Condom's efforts (q.v.).

Fertility was quite a problem in the 1600s if Mary Honeywood of Lenham, Kent is anything to go by. Her tombstone claims that she was survived by 16 children, 114 grandchildren, 228 great grandchildren and 9 great-great grandchildren.

Queen Anne produced seventeen children, which might account for the shape of her legs.

The Victorians

The vast majority of modern sexual hang-ups can be blamed on the Victorians. They were not pillars of moral rectitude. They were simply confused.

The idea that copulating was strictly for populating, that a lady performs sex as a duty not a pleasure, that masturbation leads to blindness and insanity and that unrepentent fornicators shall suffer the flames of eternal damnation are all the products of Victorian minds.

It was also Victorian minds that first brought sado-masochism and paedophilia to Britain. The late 1800s saw the heyday in London of brothels specialising in the procurement of children and the employment of corsetted whip-wenches catering for flagellation and bondage.

The Victorians found out that while abstinence made the heart grow fonder it also had some powerful effects on the libido. The need to express the male affliction led to some sweet-smelling rationalisations. 'Saving fallen women' was a common one. The position of mistress became an acceptable rôle in polite society and at the commercial end of the same spectrum the brothel-keeper was elevated to the post of Madame. In better circles she often made as great a fortune as her wealthier clients.

The Modern Era

A glimpse at the advertisements for Escort Agencies, the third page of top-selling tabloid newspapers, the queues of voyeurs in Amsterdam bookshops, the steamed-up rear windows of back-alley BMWs, the crowded waiting rooms of STD clinics and the graffiti in every end cubicle should persuade you that plus ça change, plus c'est la même chose.

GLOSSARY

Algolagnia – Clinical term for sado-masochism, the 'pleasures' derived from giving or receiving pain.

Bed – Bachelor of Education.

Bondage – The sport of kinks.

Brewer's Droop – Erectile failure when caught on the hop.

Catamite – A sodomite with two hulls.

Chordee – A fibrous band typically on the upper aspect of the penis causing the fully erect organ to take on the shape of a boomerang. Often inoperable. Sufferers usually overcome this complaint by developing a different bowling action.

Clingfilm – Roll your own condom. Not recommended.

Deep Throat – Perhaps the most famous blue movie ever made. Starring Linda Lovelace and Harry Zwilvlancz. (Get your tongue round that then.)

Detumescence – Technical term for the droop.

Diamonds – A sign of confidence in one's investment.

Duvet – A quilt complex.

Eonism – The alternative name for transvestitism. An anagram of Simeon or Simone.

Eros – Greek god of love. His Roman equivalent was Cupid.

Erotic Act – Cupid stunt.

Erotic Art – Pornography with silk underpants.

Escort – Well organised prostitute.

Exhibitionism – A display of erotic art.

Fetishism – The use of a talisman to achieve sexual arousal. The fetishist can become obsessed by a particular part of the body, a type of clothing or some other inanimate object. Obsessions with rubberwear are often seen as kinky except in scuba-divers.

Fish-net Stockings – A means of saying 'Hello Sailor' without moving the lips.

Fornication – Sexual activity.

Frottage – A covert means of achieving sexual enjoyment by rubbing up against a member of the opposite sex in a crowded place, such as a tube-train or the checkout at Tesco's. Also known, wrongly, as frotteurism.

Gay – Homosexual, whether male or female, happy or miserable. Originally a 19th century term for prostitute.

Gay Bars – What Oscar Wilde sat behind in Reading gaol.

Gigolo – Italian folk hero. Part jiggle. Part low.

Gokuraku Ojo – Death in ecstasy: sexual hara-kiri.

Gommorah – Where the Sodomites went to rest their butts.

Gooseberry Bush – Where babies came from before sex was conceived.

Guilt – The collision damage incurred when what you know to be nice coincides with what you were taught was naughty.

Headache – A pain in the neck.

Horses – Mrs Patrick Campbell, the actress friend of George Bernard Shaw, advised: 'It doesn't matter what you do in the bedroom provided you don't do it in the streets and frighten the horses.' (See also Catherine the Great.)

Love – The oldest excuse.

Love Bite – Adolescent tattoo of affection, often lasting longer than the relationship.

Masochism – The derivation of sexual pleasure from being controlled, humiliated or physically hurt by another person. The name derives from Leopald von Sacher Masoch, a failed Austrian novelist who liked being whipped.

Masturbation – In Woody Allen's words: 'Don't knock masturbation, it's making it with someone you really respect.'

Missionary Position – The Genesis chapter one of sexual experimentation.

Nymphomania – Miserable and mercifully rare condition affecting women in which the sufferer is incapable of reaching a satisfying climax but is continually driven to do so by a high libido. Accounts of the happy nympho variety are the products of immature male minds.

Pornography – Anything, anywhere, considered obscene by someone, somewhere.

Roses – Offering sent by a man to a woman shortly before, soon after or occasionally instead of, a good night out. (See also Guilt.)

Sadism – The derivation of sexual pleasure from the infliction of pain or humiliation on another creature. The name is derived from the Marquis de Sade, a rich psychopath who spent 22 years of his life in jail. Despite copious writings on his alleged propensities he was only ever found guilty of two minor offences involving sexual violence.

Satyriasis – The male equivalent of nymphomania. The sufferer is taunted by an insatiable libido and never achieves true orgasmic relief.

Sinners – Those who transgress state-of-the-art morality.

Voyeurism – More impressively known as scopophilia. Gaining sexual pleasure from watching naked bodies or sexual activity.

Wankie – A town in western Zimbabwe, population 24,000.

THE AUTHORS

Tim Webb was born in 1955 and spent most of his formative years in Birmingham, sin city of the industrial Midlands. To say that he attended Medical School there is stretching the truth somewhat but they were eventually kind enough to give him a degree on condition that he went somewhere else.

He is now a psychiatrist ministering to troubled minds in Plymouth. He has no interest whatever in treating sexual problems as he finds them all terribly embarrassing.

His greatest disappointment was puberty, which took away all his desire to open the batting for Warwickshire and replaced it with a nagging awareness that half the world is women. His main interests are self-preservation, Bathams bitter and the quest for a zipless anorak.

His connection with his co-author is purely intimate.

Sarah Brewer was born in Somerset in 1958 but moved to Cornwall for potty-training. She became so adept that in 1977 she gained a place at Selwyn College, Cambridge to study Marine Biology. She eventually qualified in Medicine, which is what happens when you stand in the wrong queue at feeding time. She now practices family doctoring in Devon and to date has doctored over fifty of them. She hopes to reach an even hundred before they catch her at it.

When not thinking about sex, she grows triffids from pips, makes wine from unlikely vegetation and enjoys intelligent conversation with sheep on Dartmoor.

She did not invent Brewer's Droop though she has known several people who might have.

THE BLUFFER'S GUIDES

Available now @ £1.00 each:

Accountancy	Music
Antiques	Paris
Class	Philosophy
Computers	Sex
Consultancy	Teaching
Golf	Television
Hi-Fi	Theatre
Hollywood	Wine
Management	

Coming, September & October 1987:

Feminism	Bluffing
Jazz	Marketing
Literature	Photography
Modern Art	Publishing

All these books are available at your local bookshop or newsagent, or can be ordered direct from the publisher. Just tick the titles you require and fill in the form below. Prices and availability subject to change without notice.

Ravette Limited, 3 Glenside Estate, Star Road, Partridge Green, Horsham, West Sussex RH13 8RA

Please send a cheque or postal order, and allow the following for postage and packing. UK 25p for one book and 10p for each additional book ordered.

Name...

Address...

....

THE BLUFFER'S GUIDES

In preparation:

Advertising
Architecture
Astrology
Ballet
Bank Managers
Beliefs
The Body
Cinema
The Classics
Defence
Espionage
Finance
Gambling
High Society
Journalism
Law
Millionaires
Opera
Politics
Property
Psychiatry

Public Relations
Secret Societies
Selling
Ski-ing
Stocks & Shares
Travel
University
World Affairs

The Americans
The Australians
The British
The French
The Germans
The Japanese

Amsterdam
Berlin
Hong Kong
Moscow
New York